Of COVID Days and More

Vivien Gomes

Contents

Musings On
Covid-19

Covid-19 At our Door

The curve needs flattening,
but people aren't listening,
to simple rules,
of isolating and distancing.

Why then moan and groan,
of the velocity of the virus?
They're in their zones,
attacking invaders in their domain.

Practise dictums of cleanliness,
have faith in your health caregivers,
there's no need to fear,
just get into gear.
Stay away from crowds,
do your best to refrain

from unnecessary,
and lurid acts of poor hygiene.

Let those who know lend us their story,
on how to conquer this state so sorry,
and get back to normality,
to breathe again creation's glory.

Daily chores,
normal socialising,
colleagues' camaraderie,
unparalleled travel,
and certainly,
freedom to move!

20 March 2020.

Our Health Care Heroes

In truth their plight,
is far from light,
starting at any unearthly hour.
There's no telling when the sirens claim,
their need to instantly intervene.

There's no excuse which demands a rest,
there's always a need for a test,
a report, or even to escort.
Stamina and presence of mind,
quick thinking and unflinching.
Their hours unusually long and dreary,
often a parched throat,
a need to answer the nudge of nature
goes unattended till who knows when.

A special day of festive cheer,

when the longing is intense to celebrate with kith and kin,

but for them it's routine.

Saving lives soothing pains,

when lives are on the line,

nothing, not one of them will decline,

to do their utmost to save, to soothe, to ease the pain.

And if support they have none,

if PPEs and all else run low,

then how can they smoothly go

caring for lives which require utmost compassion and precision?

Nurses, technicians, triage staff,

cleaners, sanitation teams,

care staff who burn the midnight oil,

to aid in the big picture,

to support saving hands.

Our consideration and support,

our understanding, concern and love,

we must offer,

as they are fragile too,
and may succumb,
to pressures due.

A mum, a dad, an offspring, a spouse,
they too are exposed,
to this deadly virus.
As we wait in expectation,
to see these weary souls come home,
after a long, long day or night of toil,
let's not forget as we salute,
the sacrifices and hardships they daily endure.

4 May 2020

An endurance certainly not for the faint-hearted.

Of Covid Days

Extraordinary days flushed with uncertainty,

all eyes constantly on newsreels and texts,

whatever could be done to allay the virus, we all did try.

And then it so chanced, those two years of care and
caution were

thrown to the wind,

as news got home that infection was rife.

A flurry of painstaking sanitation, quarantine and
pharmacy visits prevailed,

phone calls, text messages and video calls were lifeline
essentials.

Meals with care assiduously prepared,

balanced, tasty nutritious fare.

Three meals plus teas and tiffins, made up the entire
day.

The kitchen was abuzz, and so was I.
As days wore on, the bones did too.

All too soon the veils lifted and it was gone.
Sanitation efforts were stepped up,
cleansing fervent and frequent,
to wipe away every trace of the deadly enemy.
Relief and happiness prevailed, until a little while later,
enemy attacked household number two.

March 2021

A tense situation for the infected frontliner and family.

A Surreal State

Silence amid chaos,
apathy in place of sympathy,
this can't be
the same people,
who frolic and dance,
who chat and sing?

There's a lull in all of that,
since this pandemic hit the world.
China or America,
Italy, Germany and here at home too,
everyone is one-minded.
Some distressed, but most hopeful,
as they come level,
with lockdown and the Restricted
Movement Order.

Innocent kiddies enjoy this state of no pressures of
school and homework,

though they'll soon miss routine and friends, and the fun
and games

school provides.

There's a lull in the free-spirited caw of the crow,

and the more sophisticated melodies of our common
feathered friends.

Where are the robust seniors who grace our parks at the
crack of

dawn?

No music floating, no joggers panting,

there's a surreal silence all around.

The creator has spoken,

it's a time to repent,

knees bent,

in silent adoration,

resort to technology, we must,

to celebrate,

reverence and fervour as service is offered,

in familiar surrounds of abodes near and far.

We plead for compassion,

as governments convene,

for discussions and policies,

to meet new needs,

we put aside our indulgences,

as we place our hopes in His mighty hands,

to show us a way,

to alter the sway,

for infection to taper,

and life to return to shades of yesterday!

A glimpse of observations during the lockdown months.

The Sound of Sirens

Amid the piercing screams of sirens,
hearts beat in anguish,
waiting and hoping,
wishing and praying.

The queues are long,
beds are slow,
will there be one, I don't know.
How we've reached this state,
we don't know!

There's no surety,
no respite,
from fears and torments,
as sirens scream,
wheels screech,

ferrying hearts to some place,
to lay troubled minds,
giving recovery futile chance.

14 August 2021.

A New Fashion Statement

Now everyone's abuzz,

a new fashion item's trending,

thus, this furore and keen excitement prevailing.

In hues of every imaginable shade,

springing up in every shape and made by deftly creative hands,

you'll be surprised at just how they're made.

Acquiring one was oh so tricky,

as merchandise was limited and pricey,

don't worry though,

for tables are turned and you have more than you'll ever need to choose

from now.

The staid single shade to comply with regulations rule,

or there's a total black to add an air of mystery.

Anyway, it's the function they provide,

and that's precisely what matters.

Creative minds soon got busy,

fashion houses and individuals

rose to the challenge to create attractive substitutes

in pretty prints, polka dots in bold hues replacing the dull greys and greens,

and creations in crimsons and pinks flooded the stores.

What a lift,

in times adrift,

to see these creations in our midst.

The Rangoli motifs, Calico stripes and animal prints vie,

for the label of haute couture.

While batiks and authentic Iban Pua cause a stir among the folk,

do print your very own signature style.

Have you heard that creative E-inventors are rocking their world?

Gaiters and super creative bejewelled pieces abound for the digital bold,

while functions remain

to protect wearer and keep out infection.

The fairer sex however moan,

their artistic made-up faces hide behind these masks, they groan.

But be consoled,

the eyes, souls to the world,

stand out, bright and dramatic,

carefully, extravagantly, staged,

1 July 2020

As this trend continues and time demands their use, the authorities worry about the effective function this vital piece of personal protection offers.

Lesson in Love

Peering intently,

the piece lying forlornly,

should the urge to abandon prevail?

Good question!

The temptation is strong, but perseverance holds,

and so, the industrious mind goes on.

Tapestry at its best,

to adorn a corner or a surface,

perhaps a little gift of love,

or simply framed for fame.

The slow pace seems conducive,

board games and handicraft items appear,

decoupage or art journaling,

pottery, weaving, Turkish upholstery,

there's delight in abundance,

derived from art forms of yore.

The old dusty violin stuffed in the trusty trunk,

finds an eager player,

all set to woo his audience,

while the reluctant teen finds peace in drumming.

Families adore,

time uninterrupted,

no annoying school bells, no urgency,

enjoying every moment of

togetherness, pampering, loving it all.

Gardens sprouting, hedges pruned while

abandoned odd jobs are getting attention.

Voila! A shed for orchid blooms, built within a day

with help from ever willing junior hands.

Mamas are springing culinary surprises,

who'd've thought eclairs and pavlovas could grace daily meals,

or that exquisite Basque burnt cheesecake could be ours to taste?

When all's done,
there's time for worship.
Have we loved the virtual services offered,
as we long for spiritual nourishment
from preachers,
near and far?

Kiddies concentrating while mums and dads their input give,
this time has brought us closer to kith and kin,
to old friends and neighbours.
Lend a hand, spread the love,
time is on our hands.

That email connection,
that unhurried telephone call,
weren't we supposed to connect,
before the pandemic struck?
It's never too late,
to bring a smile, to bring good cheer,
to friends and family so very dear.

Many households embraced the lockdown as a time to bond.

The Evasive Enemy

Writhing, squirming, pulsing, being,
Unrelenting, scheming.
Infiltrating every imaginable crevice,
surface, corner, border.
Conquering tens, thousands, millions.

In serene settings, in deep jungles,
on minute surfaces,
in crowds, and company,
there isn't a spot they haven't conquered.

With outstretched hands with sorrowful pleas,
food for the family,
sustenance for the soul.
Terror, worry, tears,
will nothing conquer this enemy?

Tens of thousands parched,

expectantly waiting for a glimpse of relief,

let not our spirits fray,

send us a solution without delay.

As floundering economies search,

for answers, for justice.

The learned and informed are baffled

while unreasonable claims abound,

we wait with bated breath,

for a close to this dismal, living death.

When hope can resume,

when we can consume,

pure and fresh abundance of this earth,

without a thought or fear,

of this intimidating,

violating,

trespassing,

tiny, puny, invisible, menacing,

enemy!

The World on Lockdown

The pendulum swings,

time surges,

a cure is sought for the evasive virus.

Distant though it sounds,

we hope there's an instant surprise,

when researchers appear with breaking news for all to hear and loudly

cheer.

Meanwhile the storm rages,

while nations shut down.

The pandemic is full-blown with numbers soaring,

with tales of the inevitable losses,

that awaken emotions and strains of despair.

Handouts and financial packages to ease burdens,

community volunteers put their best foot forward,

to touch the hearts of seniors and the downtrodden too.

Our gallant healthcare workers meanwhile,

unflinching,

sacrificing,

working relentlessly,

to ease, to care, to cure.

Many are

mums and dads,

wrenched from their little ones,

to help, to ease the plight of the sick in their care.

Walking down history's epidemics and plagues,

this scourge equates to the

Spanish flu of the 20th century,

claiming lives and paralysing economics.

Yellow fever and Typhus, and more recently H1N1,

the Zika virus and the Ebola too,

but Corona now is our taboo.

Governments must be transparent,
without downplaying issues
for their own selfish reasons.
Intelligentsia must act quickly,
as more and more,
succumb to
gloom and depression.

We gaze at horizons with expectation,
with adherence to advice from psychologists and physicians,
and hope that it keeps minds active,
lest we fall into highly volatile experiences,
resulting from dire circumstances.

Is This Real?

A challenging situation,
we are all in it,
frayed nerves, sinking emotions,
who can change the course of things,
unless we together try.
There are SOPs to be adhered to,
much to be changed,
but unless we try,
who's going to slide?
Outrageous numbers prevail,
desperate measures put into place,
but if we don't try, who will?

The deluge of articles,
videos and text messages on the pandemic are
enough to fill your plate,

numerous agencies and hundreds of individuals
clamour for relief,

but what's all this for,

if basic principles are not upheld?

And What Now?

As numbers drop,
as frontiers are lifted, albeit slowly,
new norms they say,
are here to stay.

If retail therapy is your thing,
if hair salons, spas and manicures your fling,
a pub run so dearly missed,
karaoke joints and sports event severed,
feel the void, oh yes.
For although the coasts seem clear,
and the green light is here,
no activity can we embrace,
with total good cheer.

For lurking surreptitiously around,
this tiny intruder hovers,

heaving, breathing, silently, seething,
to snatch its glorious crown of notoriety.

So tread we must so cautiously,
practising every act of personal protection,
within the home, at work and play,
lest we again fall prey.

No, no one wants to slip into the grips,
of that agony,
that feeling of despondency,
wherein the daily throes of fear and bondage,
all life's activities must revolve.

Let's throw up our hands,
and face the sky,
full days to enjoy,
tracing footsteps in the sand,
stealing moments of joy,
enjoying camaraderie without
the nagging fear or doubt of a stark tomorrow.

The Aftermath

As the pandemic is now an endemic,
the fever is slowly sliding,
rules are bending,
there's never enough of anything.

Pop-ups are everywhere,
sale of items,
here and there,
is there no end
to restaurants, pubs,
and even more clubs?

Society is caught up in building
losses and keeping promises,
young families,

yearn for days past,
when cash was boss.

For many,
it's a new start,
to renew, rebuild to fortify,
and as this frenzy escalates,
there's more to ponder,
is life's quality compromised,
aren't we becoming too eager?

Consciously consider,
before you venture,
stringent parameters to keep.
When planning and preparing,
avoid shortcuts and empty promises.
Give of your fullest, always,
the rewards await the best.

Irrelevance

In most corners where the virus was rife,

*folks seemed eager to work together to face
the intruder.*

*No dramatic resistance to restrictions, to outsmart
the enemy,*

instead, a strong bond prevailed

to claim good sense and to continue life's journey.

*For twenty-four months and more,
nations continued to struggle*

to find a cure,

to end the war.

In good time we found vaccines and their efficacy,

while sceptical minds questioned,

the world largely complied.

When the pandemic was termed endemic,
a noticeable change we could see.
Apprehension and the docile acceptance
turned to unsavoury loathings,
edged with despondency and a sense of
apparent disdain.

Entitled youth, questioning seniors,
undisciplined teens and tots
resulted in many societies.

This display of arrogance and notoriety
shows its fangled claws and the making of a world of
irrelevance
and a rabid obsession to challenge authority.

March 2024

*A reaction to the world's view after the worst days of the
pandemic.*

People, Places
and
Events

A Leap of Sorts

A leap of sorts was sought,
at the turn of the millennium,
a leap so huge,
a turning point,
a point of no return.

And so the plan began
to seek a route,
sans too much pain,
alternating from trepidation, to serious apprehension,
indeed, a huge move to eventuate.

The hunt began for suitable tertiary facilities,
wondering and considering,
the most suitable paths of education for
the young ladies.

There lay other big considerations too.
An abode to secure,
employment opportunities and most importantly,
a seamless move for the dear aged parents.

With all this done,
the move seemed feasible.
A half move was achieved, and then the full.

The thrill of new surrounds,
across the South China Sea, a new work environment,
a first-time experience of condo living with the extra
thrill of big city life beckoned.

Two graduations,
two weddings, our hall of fame proudly displays,
but the icing on the cake?
Our four precious darlings!

And life goes on,
the evening of life's beginnings approach,
achieving a calm, and graciously unique

lifetime of peace and doing
the best for selves and the rest.

All's well that ends well,
but at times the heart still yearns for
unbeatable, carefree, wholesome days of life's first love,
The Land Below the Wind.

January 2000

The move from a land well-loved to the bright lights of
the city.

Those were the days

They were days of diapers and endless toys,
of sleepless nights and toddlers' ploys.
For childhood ailments, home remedies I'd try,
skilfully administered,
before the doc walked in!

Then there was the day-to-day war with self,
would Atkins or the Mediterranean diet
do the trick?
Quick, before the years creep on
and seams seemed to get to bursting point,
shouldn't I be able to revel in clothes and shoes in shop windows displayed
of which
the heart so desired?

Absorbed in self-glorification
when time allowed,
'twas happiness,
to this weary expectant soul.
If online shopping was then the norm,
right on board I would have been.
Instead, scouring malls was priority,
with or without company.

When years crept on
and growing teens took me by storm,
mood swings and demands were a trying thing.
While steadily keeping pace,
with imparting knowledge and grading
endless papers at work,
these two precious lives I had to shield,
from contagions of the world,
while nurturing minds so young.

And now in retrospect,
the race must go on,
to pick up what was undone.

Well, the season's just right,
no mall crawls,
no gym trips, and the inevitable
chats and lunches to follow,
just home-bound satisfaction,
and quiet times in spiritual adoration.

Forced confinement has brought waves of wonder,
to friends and family.
Threading a needle is no more a chore,
even the garden's yielding more!
Why, the greens are ever so lush,
while flowering creations flourish
amidst a lime tree and even a bed of herbs!

Recipes are tried with gusto,
to the delight of friends and family.
Dear Mercy's "moru kachi" is perfected,
while Marie's "inji puli" is mastered.
If Kurshid and Martine chanced to taste their
crème caramel recipe,
they'd give me a hearty nod, I know.

Michele's French baguette and pâté are next in line,
wait and see if they'll taste fine.

And yes, the solitude has evoked,
thoughts to flow,
so here's the show.
The pen has been busy,
my friends, as you all now know.

17 November 2020

In response to my friends who wonder how I kept under wraps
this writing activity in our early days of friendship!

moru kachi - A light seasoned buttermilk curry
inji puli - A sweet and tangy ginger relish

Forever Love

A heart of silver and precious gold,
huge lashings of sunshine and laughter,
a pile of wisdom,
several tons of understanding and,
understated patience
that's what you are.

Through many trials and woes,
through heartbreaks and joys,
mother is your best friend, your first friend,
your rock.

You're forever embraced,
in this warm and perfect glow,
so show your eternal love,
your dedication,

your purest form of appreciation.

Your life, your heartfelt

thanks,

immense gratitude,

forever love.

Weathered hands and knobbly fingers,

face etched with a thousand rivers

of silent tears, heart breaks,

yet, no one ever suffers

the wrath of a most loved mother forever.

She hides them well,

in tears that swell,

in deep pouches of her eyes' darkest wells.

That silver edging, or mostly gold,

tells that all's well.

In her pride and joy, she embraces the glories well,

thanking her creator in sacred prayer,

seizing every moment to lead her offsprings,

in light of grace,
as He created her to be.

The unconditional love of mothers.

A True Friend

In days past when the weight of the world burdened,
a state of mind too saddened,
by grief and fear,
you were always near,
a rock of wisdom and strength,
a call away was where you were.

You've weathered your share of storms,
but unwavering is your faith,
so nothing, none will destroy that peace,
and calm reassuring,

A seasoned chef,
to whom only perfection would suffice,
if there's a tiny flaw,
how lovingly will you ponder,
every avenue before you finally let it rest.

Many have encountered your dogmatic views,

in search of perfection.

Doctors, lawyers, accountants, actuaries,
religious, the lot,

are your precious followers.

for in them did you instil,

the finite intricacies of Mathematics,

served with loads of love and laughter,

and oftentimes a grimace or two,

so tardy tykes could be forewarned.

Hospitable and accomplished,

you'd reverse a drab room,

and in a trice convert it to a home with artistic
touches aplenty,

reflected in your abode, so cosy.

Above all a woman of deep faith you are,

how can I thank you for your generous spirit, your
unquestioning candour,

so often claimed at unearthly hours of the day?

Though seas divide,
no one can snatch the hotline between us away.
Live well your golden years,
embrace the rich friendships your community provides,
lending your ear to every soul,
who in want of solace, turns to one so giving of self.

An ode to a special friend.

The Gem at the Corner

The gem at the corner
stands proud and strong,
a reminder of hours of pleasure,
your lasting and fond signature.

After two score years or more,
of juggling mind-boggling numbers and
finicky fractions,
of endless stacks of paper and bulging files,
of responsibilities with no distractions,
this endeavour is a soothing walk in the park.

Now the sweet days of rest and recreation yield,
green finger-magic, a latent desire,
a deep want to propagate nature.

Halcyon days beckon change,

a change welcome to the eye.

If roses and hydrangea,

were a past passion,

now purple ruellia and snow lilies are the fashion.

A delight to the senses to behold,

more greens and lantanas in hues so bold,

dance in unison with ornamental chilli,

and wild ginger shoots,

plump tomatoes for the table, and slender okra too.

In this sweet haven to treasure,

for years of pleasure,

beyond measure.

Indulgence sublime,

fragrances pure,

this is where your energies find release.

A friend's latent desire realised.

Déjà vu

If Déjà vu is the name for the feeling, then bring it on!
The buntings and decor bring to mind days of yore,
transported to these moments when not
so many aeons ago
mamma and aunt brought the same intense
waves of emotions.

Proud and fearless, calm yet confident
both generations hold high the flag of valour and dignity.
Go Lizzie into the unknown,
traverse worlds awaiting
without trepidation or worry,
The Lord is your light
As you reach for the stars shimmering bright.

6 September 2019
A moment of pride, captured.

We Three Kings

As the strains of 'We Three Kings of Orient
Are' filled the air,

I naturally went into mode reminisce I declare.

Decades ago, the drama teacher had a bee in
her bonnet

to train a handful of her wards

to do parts of the nativity.

Angel of the Sun was designated,

and with it came relentless hours of off-school
rehearsals,

weekends, term breaks and all.

The day finally arrived and you guessed it,

what a winner it was!

There, was born the seeds of stage shows...
except of course with roles
reversed.

And as this year begins,

there will not be opportunities of directing
a production,

but fond memories of the many past
episodes remain.

The toil, endless hours of worry,

made up for the end result, with delirious
accolades and final encore!

The youthful exuberance of my crew,

and most importantly the stars, were unforgettable
moments!

Why, several years hence, there was one of
my special stars

who having expertly played "Charlie" in Flowers
for Algernon

introduced himself as a

successful dental surgeon in town!

Unexpected confidence,
suave grace and untold wisdom,
a result of exposure and hours
of unparalleled inspiration to excel,
made fine people of these tender hearts.

Re-living the days of stage.

A Night of Terror

Silhouettes scream,

walls turn wild,

torrents of congealed blood and slime cover
every corner, every crevice,

is there no end to this agony?

As twisted

gnarled fingers trace brows with perspiration,

in among the tangled green,

huge moans and sighs prevail,

in the darkest, eerie night.

Then stately struts the night owl,

with practiced precision, accompanying
the symphony,

in the deepest depths of the night,

gingerly pacing, hardly breathing.

A paralysing screech jolts the mind,
and pretty soon all is well, sans misery,
sans fear, sans mystery.

Painting pictures in the mind.

A Task at ASK

As chatter escalates and deft hands get busy,
as knives and peelers get furiously noisy,
all eyes are focused on tasks,
to get the first of many cauldrons bubbling merrily.

A tiny group sits serious,
heads bent, knives poised,
to undertake a less loved chore,
tackling tear-jerking,
onions, and less intense,
but more pungent ginger,
and sidekick, garlic.

A break well earned, rewarded with a hot cuppa
and an array of snacks healthy, though at times no,
signals one of many jobs done.
After all, the dozen or two golden gals and guys,

having spent decades analysing their ills,
decide on a happy cocktail,
of what to eat and what to skip,
with no specifics, none at all.

A bond so special, one that transcends boundaries,
easy conversations, light-hearted jibes,
in peaceful reassurance
bathed in our Saviour's gaze.

Come Mondays and Wednesdays,
the joy that follows each session is priceless,
as scores of hungry mouths are fed,
and happy smiles evoked.

There's no joy quite so sublime,
nothing so divine,
as the endless possibilities,
extended to hopeful hearts,
nourishing tired bodies,
and lifting countless spirits.

In humble gratitude and a thousand unspoken words,

toothless grins speak volumes,

expressing thanks, thus

tugging at heartstrings, urging, nudging,

to continue to give of selves to a cause oh so rewarding.

May 2019

Volunteer work at the soup kitchen.

Hag, oh no!

Sunny days of youthful wanton escapades,
of silly spills and mighty thrills.
Here I come, hag or no,
wisdom wrought from experience,
bejewelled in compassion,
random blessings caught
in lines, folds or cracks.

Do I worry?
Oh yes!

Of days to come and life's surprises to bear,
but nowhere, not anywhere does the soul lack,
fortitude to go easy,
breathe, savour, tease.

Here I come, warts, flab and all,

to live, to love and to endure,

every straw life has in store!

20 September 2022

A candid reaction to a controversy.

A Delightful Trove

No unusual fanfare,
only solid ware,
there's no telling if you'd miss the store,
cos of the nondescript door.

Enter and you'll be amazed at what's in store,
from "good morning" towels
of the past, to everything under the sun,
you'll find it in this put-together treasure trove!
If it's a stationery item of the past you need,
or if a penchant for Mum's old kitchen stove you long,
beads and baubles, shoes of yore,
or even a haberdashery need, it's all in store.

Teaching aids and foot rugs,
and a longing for those enamel mugs?
There's always a chance for your needs here, do not fear.

A chance encounter did we have,

with the proprietor of this treasure trove

and what wonderful stories ensued.

From life in China to how this treasure began,

by a staid, yet humble soul, we were entertained.

In such a place as this,

One tends to linger,

when all's done and two grinning ladies hunt,

for a delectable bowl of "tau fu fah".

Such a feast for the eyes, this place is.

Up a narrow flight with treasures laden and feet swollen,

We'd have the best treat in this cosy retreat.

A chance discovery, well-loved.

Sera

Determined and self-reliant,
trusting and lovable,
at times a tad quirky,
a kind soul who put herself last,
that was our dear Sera.

She filled the space with cheer,
seeing to every need in her sphere,
tongue-in-cheek jokes she served,
to eager ears around to savour,
oh, how we miss you, dear Sera.

Compassion and duty took her places,
no fear, no hesitation.
From Cheras to Puchong she'd go,

and then to Bukit Nanas and back,
in the most unearthly hour,

to ease, to cheer and to comfort,

weary hearts in deep despair.

Her generosity of time knew no bounds,

everything was a possibility, nothing out of
her reach.

God's creations you protected,

the birds had their share, and the felines too,

while to amuse the kids she'd take

the loveliest gifts and treats she could afford.

The Lord's trusted handmaid,

Sera you truly enshrined the gospel,

a woman of deep faith and simplicity,

there's none that will forget your selfless
acts of charity.

Rest thee well in the arms of your creator,

no more worry, no sadness, no sickness you
need endure,

in the Saviour's embrace you are secure.

Farewell dear friend, you will be missed
for the ray of hope you brought into
many a heart you did assist.

10 August 2021

A tribute to Sera - a cherished friend at the soup kitchen.

Sheila

A beacon in the night,
she brought life to light,
a practical being,
but wait, there's no fooling,
she called a spade a spade, not
tolerating weaklings!

Countless are her acts of kindness,
and innumerable friends grieve
the passing of a lovely lady,
we all had the fortune of knowing.

Her interests were many,
she did not tarry.
In a jiffy she'd cook up a curry,
or be a relief to the weary.
Nothing was a chore to her,

but don't take the wrath of this lovely
creature lightly,
or she'll tell you exactly where you belong!

Her witty demeanour, and instant
gregarious laughter could stun a room
or even leave you spellbound with
her belting out the latest song.

No airs or reserve, she captured all,
living a life so full, and loving it all.

What a void this passing brings,
her kith and kin are numb with grief,
as are we who mourn with them.

You had a mission up above,
and you went to undertake it
with your usual gusto,
so how could we say no?

Rest in the arms of Jesus dear Sheila,
with our tears and hearts full of sadness,
we bid you our last farewell.

6 February 2020
To a beloved lady.

A Whisper in Daylight

A wisp of a woman waltzed in
head held high and proud,
a definite air of confidence,
a certain air of quintessential charm she held,
a sunhat of sorts framed her nearly perfect chiseled
features,
affording charm and poise
for the eye to behold.

Her air of grace surpassed all
as she scrolled the menu with complete ease.
Age defying, though signs showing,
an easy seventy or even a close eighty,
how regal was her air as she persevered.

All of that little lithe body leaving
gracefully was a perfect sight,

fully satiated with her frugal meal
and now a sprightly walk across the park
which led her to her humble abode.

A chance meeting at the same spot weeks later,
her favourite respite it proved to be
now examining with a trained and exacting eye,
nature's bounties at store next door.

If semblance of grace,
charm and elegance were interchanged
with grumpy, crotchety and unapproachability,
that'd be her.
Now, this vision so perfect was far from
the epitome of the genteel nature she'd portrayed.

A study in reality.

As We Await

When another day has passed,
when all of '22 is done and dusted,
when the night bird sings of the morning's glory,
then shall we invite the bright new day,
clinging on to the cusp of fragility,
in revered hush
as lives lie open, waiting
for what the new year brings.

Arid days, waiting on His divine will,
for the skies to open forth,
spilling its bounty on mortals,
who wait agape for what's to come.

We welcome the new day with grateful hearts,
as beyond yonder we peer,
to straighten every curve,

to enlighten every soul,

and to bring a change so great,

that you and yours may embrace a brand-new world,

a new acceptance,

a new tomorrow for us and ours.

31 December 2022

On the eve of the new year of 2023.

Humble Gratitude

She strode in cheerily,
the corridor hit cold and severely,
a light breeze she breathed when she waved a hello.
Dumbstruck by her warmth,
I nodded at this unexpected gesture.

The figure cut a confident posture
in subdued colours beneath her protective armour.
Already a little thawed by this friendly countenance
the call came a lot less icy.

When into the foreboding door I was escorted,
to where the glare of lights and a staid examination
bed stood,
on which future alternatives to life may possibly be
declared.
Again, a bright welcome as on the bed I lay

waiting to hear the verdict of the day.

No unnecessary jargon, no airs,

*just sensible small talk and pleasantries to ease
the stretched nerves.*

All clear!

Sweetest words in a while surely, to the ear.

*Days of agony and tears wiped away with those
soothing words.*

Music to my ears delivered by you

solid yet soft, professional yet compassionate.

If social distancing was not the call of the day

A warm hug would have come your way.

January 2019

Recalling a happy turn of events.

Ouch!

It just doesn't stop!
Thoughts keep whirling and churning,
wondering how on earth it happened.
How can a calm innocuous action have resulted
in such a trigger of
emotions!

The day was calm, insipid duties to be
accomplished at home, a serene
setting, then what?
Three months later when a related incident
came round, perhaps some light
began to unravel.
That inner ear, how or what it looks like
matters little,
it's the potent danger that dwells within it,
that matters.

This unfortunate fall caused damage to skin,

again, harmless enough,

but resulted in moments of utter distress for
one so alien to pain!

A five-stitch repair was made to hold
together skin asunder.

There was such a rush of adrenaline that
I was indeed stunned.

Precise and determined and against all
Hippocratic Oaths,

an exception to that rule had to be made.

Lo and behold,

a familiar face was above mine,

thrown into a crease-filled study in
concentration.

The job had to be done under dire
circumstances,

and done it had to be, to perfection.

Needless, to say, the nursing aides were
victims of severe hand twisting

and sweaty palms, but in twenty minutes flat,

I was all cleaned up and packed off!

4 February 2022

One of those things I endured.

Vision 20/20

As weeks and days slipped by,

and days of apprehension staggered to a halt,

the long anticipated Covid test before the actual storm arrived

bright and early on the 4th day of the 9th month

of the year twenty twenty-three.

Before dawn crept in,

was I ready to charge to hospital

where awaited the dreaded test,

more dreaded than the actual deed!

As counter Number 7 called my name I sped up with false courage only to be

told that the test was now obsolete!

A sigh of deep relief ensued,

but the poor reception clerk was victim of my wrath,

as I told him that I was put to

unnecessary worry for three long months after
the date was set, and no notification had I received
otherwise!

One more night of agony, as 5th September dawned
and off to hospital I was seen.
The waiting was minimal and formalities done,
I was tucked in bed in the
daycare wing of the sterile facility.
No sooner had I got my head around my thoughts
as to wait or to disappear,
the calm and collected voice of the doctor was in my ear.

From that moment there was no turning back
as I was soon wheeled into the minor OT.
No restraining limbs did I embarrass myself with,
but docile as a lamb to the slaughter,
gave in to that procedure which many had
persuaded me to conquer.

And minutes later... was it ten or fifteen,

I was smack into the thick of it,

slightly emotional, largely brave.

Voila, the deed was done and within the next ten,

was swung around expertly to my earlier nook!

The absolutely tasty beverage

which deserved no second mention,

came in a warm cup... heavenly, creamy and chocolatey,

'twas just what the distressed, but calmed soul needed.

5 September 2024

A dreaded day which turned out surprisingly smooth.

Where Similarity Ends

While tinkling bells and battery-operated toys
vie for attention,

the soft strokes of street art take precedence.

The finest talent displayed in intricate detail

tourists battle sweltering heat eyeing designs
on walls and street corners.

A sultry day, just ideal to breathe in

the aroma of a mixed heritage,

of oh so western temptations

to delight the palate

side by side with heady aromas of
home-grown staples.

Making a decision seems disloyal, but

whither the senses roam,

the soul indulges.

Be it "char kwey teow" in a coffee shop regular,

or sipping chocolate laced liqueur in a
fancy gem set

in the depths of a colonial home,

That's the Pearl of the Orient for you.

And that's where the similarity ends

with beloved hometown across enchanting
South China Sea.

While Carpenter Street and Satok Road seem

quaint and ancient like sister city,

and Hokkien is lingua franca in both
beloved regions,

Cat city has succumbed to the mangled
hands of steel and glass.

Simple pretty lanes have been smothered
by high-rise giants

to seriously compete in the game of
competitive development.

Alas, shouldn't there have been
thought given

before the mighty giants attacked?

Kuching beckons anyway, so here I come
a visit long overdue to revel in its glory of
way back when.

A comparison of two beloved cities.

Thai Delights

No dizzying heights,

no screeching wheels,

the peaceful chaos that surrounds the streets,

is a sight indeed to behold.

A walk along the clean yet crowded streets,

devoid of mayhem and chaos,

a welcome delight to the senses.

In the distance lofty temples stand,
as bells tinkling,

their splendour spreading,

to the little town at the isthmus.

Fast forward, the hotel affords an oasis
to weary travellers.

Staff are the epitome of hospitality

and their soft and empathetic demeanour

is beyond compare.
When an emergency strikes,
Thai hospitality prevails.
With dexterity and intent,
hotel staff get into quick action,
soothing the distressed with care and utmost
compassion.

Food abounds,
sea creatures of all descriptions,
cost but a third so all limitations are forgotten,
when swarmed with them.
Foot and body massages take precedence,
who'd've thought that a pint-sized masseuse's quiet
strength could unlock
tired knotted sinews and rejuvenate the entire being?

Creamy Thai mango desserts in various hues
juxtaposition with enormous lobsters
and other roadside wonders,
assaulting the senses,
making dinnertime dreams a reality.

People are alike everywhere, and yet so different.
Where feverish chaos and pandemonium is common
back home,
'tis the picture of calm and decorum here,
even from the simple folk around.

Undeterred by sophistication,
simple, soft, unaffected banter is heard.
The company was perfect,
camaraderie enjoyed,
like-minds met with warmth,
with graciousness around,
unforced, no extremes, always
considerate, peace filled and light-hearted.

Train ride was smooth,
planning was perfect.
The loot is aplenty,
but there's more to come,
when friends are a calling,
for a repeat of the trip soonest.

The Art of Perfection Defined

When dinner's done and the night bird calls,
alone in the study,
pouring over copious piles,
in mixed bundles and files,
sits a head bent in utmost concentration.

And where's that smile and loud guffaw?
There's business to be done,
there's no time for fun,
no after dinner drives,
less banter,
until the fever,
is done and over.

A word amiss,
a phrase out of place,

little escapes this meticulous soul,

until it's done to precision.

Had age been kinder,

a change in profession,

might he consider?

January 2023

*Observation on the other half working on secretary's
minutes of a social club.*

www.ingramcontent.com/pod-product-compliance
Lightning Source LLC
Chambersburg PA
CBHW021121130726
47988CB00003B/1110